T0129861

Discovery

IS

Recovery

BRAIN, EMOTION, AND SPIRITUAL
SELF-REFLECTION THROUGH
THE CREATIVE PROCESS

BRENDA L BALDING MA

BALBOA.PRESS
A DIVISION OF HAY HOUSE

Balboa Press books may be ordered through booksellers or by contacting:

Balboa Press
A Division of Hay House
1663 Liberty Drive
Bloomington, IN 47403
www.balboapress.com
844-682-1282

Print information available on the last page.

ISBN: 979-8-7652-3355-9 (sc)
ISBN: 979-8-7652-3356-6 (hc)
ISBN: 979-8-7652-3354-2 (e)

Library of Congress Control Number: 2022915954

Balboa Press rev. date: 11/02/2022

I dedicate my "Discovery Is Recovery" Focused Journals to all on a self-awareness journey who are open to discover their brain-emotion-spirit connection.

To Err Is Human

You may find errors or typos in this book. Please know that they do serve a purpose. The author wanted to write something for everyone, and some "brains" enjoy—even revel—in ferreting out mistakes.

Publisher's Reminder

Any journey starts with the first step, some scholars say. For me it starts with being willing to learn and discover who I am, to be my true authentic self. The journey you are about to begin may be a true adventure of discovery for you. Enjoy the ride.

Color the black-and-white pictures throughout as you choose. More "Discovery Is Recovery" Focused Journals are coming soon.

CONTENTS

FOREWORD

If I had to describe the impetus behind Brenda's envisioning a set of journals, it would be the benefits of self-awareness. This involves a personal knowledge of one's own character, thoughts, emotions, feelings, desires, and motives, along with a knowledge of how one is viewed by others. Although many believe they have high self-awareness, studies estimate that only one in ten to fifteen individuals really possess those skills with accuracy. This speaks to the old proverb that you cannot take steps to get out of a trap if you do not even realize you are in one.

Did you know that the essential life skills of emotional intelligence (EQ) and self-awareness are linked hand in glove? They are linked because building EQ skills requires strong self-awareness. If one is self-unaware, it will likely be difficult, if not impossible, to recognize behaviors that could be changed, improved, or created by raising one's level of EQ skills.

The research shows that emotional intelligence skills are worth 80 percent of one's overall success in life per Daniel Goleman, while IQ contributes a mere 20 percent. That gives you a glimpse into where you might want to put your time and energy.

Self-awareness, while critically important, is a slippery slope, requiring an honest commitment to personal evaluation. For example, in almost any hierarchy, people considered the higher-ups are the least likely to be aware of how others perceive them. Why? Because there are fewer individuals above to provide kind and helpful feedback, while those below may be unwilling to take the risk.

There are ways in which you can consciously increase your self-awareness.

- Pay attention in the moment to what is happening both inside you and in your environment. Imagine watching yourself from the outside, monitoring your appearance and behaviors, and noting how they influence your interactions and relationships.
- Learn to identify your emotions quickly and accurately, determine their likely triggers, and discover the information they want to share with you. Perhaps you can take steps to heal and release some emotional baggage.
- Realize that your brain creates your feelings from its interpretation of how you respond to your emotions and the importance you place on the information they are attempting to give you. Know that to change the way you feel, you must change the way you think.
- Be open to feedback. View solicited or unsolicited comments dispassionately. They are, after all, only another brain's *opinion.* However, you can become more self-aware of your behaviors by knowing how they are perceived, at least by some. There's always something you can learn.
- Avoid why questions (e.g., Why did I say/do that?), which lead to rationalization. Instead, ask what questions (e.g., What steps must I take to avoid these less-than-desirable behaviors in the future?).

- Hang out with self-aware individuals; they can help you sharpen your skills. Treat others as you would prefer to be treated. What you circulate into the environment often comes back to you.
- Choose to journal. It can be enlightening to see what emerges on the page in front of you, especially if you try writing with your nondominant hand. Studies suggest that this is one way to contact your vast subconscious, which includes an estimated 80 percent of your brain and your entire body.

Building self-awareness skills can help you build emotional intelligence skills. These two essential life skills are linked, which brings us back to journaling, that can help you become more self-aware.

Because Brenda has learned this in her own life, she has put in the thought, time, and energy to create journals that can help you become more self-aware too.

Some say, "Journaling isn't my thing." That may be true. Not all brains march to the same drum. However, it could be more helpful than you might imagine, especially as you are not simply facing a blank page when you use one of Brenda's Focused Journals. Think of it as a helpful tool to use in your own journey of self-awareness. I wonder what you may discover. You may be surprised!

Arlene R. Taylor, PhD
Founder and president of Realizations Inc. www.arlenetaylor.org

Brenda L Balding, MA

Some activities can provide you with a different and more powerful access to your brain.

Write or draw with your nondominant hand to potentially enhance self-reflection by accessing the subconscious.

This guide includes other tools for brain-emotion-spirit exploration. They may expand or enrich your life experience. Embrace your own journey of discovery.

INTRODUCTION

Arlene and some of my peers encouraged me to create a series of journals that use my photographs, thought-provoking quotes, my personal experience, and a variety of ways in which to explore the brain-emotion-spirit connection. My hope is that you enjoy the journey. For me, self-discovery is vital, interesting, healing—and it can be fun!

Travel has enriched my brain, emotions, and spiritual way of being in the world. Discovering foreign countries as well as inner exploration. I have learned that what distinguishes *Homo sapiens* (humans) from every other living creature is the mind, which the brain creates during gestation, and which can eventually affect and direct the brain that formed it. Consensus seems to be that whatever else human beings are, we are relational, sexual/emotional, and spiritual. Each may choose to write their own stories as they become more self-aware.

Sometimes people get nervous about the word *spiritual* and even confuse it with *religious*. They are separate entities that may be experienced together, separately, or one without the other. So that we are all on the same page, here are my definitions of *spirituality* and *religion*.

Spirituality is the spirit with which you live life, including ethical or moral choices, mindfulness, and core beliefs. It may involve an inner sense of something greater than yourself, a higher power or inner knowing, the recognition of a meaning to existence that transcends today's human circumstances. Spirituality may include a sense of awe, vision, or goals to achieve the highest possible levels of brain-body-spirit health and wellness. Some refer to spirituality as another type of intelligence.

Choosing to show up each day with compassion, acceptance, and willingness to be open to learn, listen, and expand self-awareness means I am living a spiritual life.

Religion is an affiliation with an organization or group espousing specific theologies or beliefs. A person can be religious without being very spiritual or can be very spiritual without being religious or aligned with a specific denomination or theology.

For those who choose to affiliate with a religion, the ideal may be that first they are spiritual. Then they choose to join an organization espousing spiritual beliefs that resonate with their brains and inner knowing.

Your brain can only do what it thinks it can do—and it is your job to tell it what it can do. Studies have shown that there is an effective way to talk to your brain. Use your first name, the pronoun *you*, and positive present-tense instructions. Talk to your brain as if it is a separate entity—which it sort of is. There are places in each chapter for you to self-talk to your brain (for example, "Brenda, you enjoy creating this series of books"). Sometimes you may need to use self-talk to help the brain correct its course.

Listening to what your brain, emotions, and spirit have to say may help you course correct as well. Learn to listen on all levels. Discover what they may have to say about a given word. Your brain talks to you through your thoughts, feelings, and inner knowing, giving you new ways of looking at life and living.

These books encourage brain-emotion-spirit connection for self-reflection and discovery—to discover yourself and how you wish to be present in the world. The words book and journal are used interchangeably. You are documenting your thoughts and feelings and creating your own story or book at the same time. Go through this journal/book in any order that works for your brain and spirit. There is no one right way. Have fun coloring the pictures as you wish.

Above all, revel in your adventure of self-reflection and self-awareness in the "Discovery Is Recovery" Focused Journals. Think about your perception of who you are as a unique human being. Notice the guests you may meet along the way.

The Guest House

This being human is a guest house.
Every morning a new arrival.

A joy, a depression, a meanness, some momentary
awareness comes as an unexpected visitor.

Welcome and entertain them all
Even if they're a crowd of sorrows, who
violently sweep your house empty of its
furniture, still, treat each guest honorably.
He may be clearing you out for some new delight.

The dark thought, the shame, the malice, meet
them at the door laughing, and invite them in.

Be grateful for whoever comes because each
has been sent as a guide from beyond.

—Rumi

Be open and honest about the reflections you experience in your mirror and those mirrored by others toward you. Pause, breathe, listen, and have fun. Think about who you are as a unique human being.

> The greatest advantage of speaking the truth is that you don't have to remember what you said.
>
> —Unknown

HONESTY

Honesty continues to be my hardest and most rewarding way of being and thinking. It is so easy to rationalize, talk story to look good, and leave honesty and wisdom behind. Being honest gets me out of should, if only or try and moves me into truth.

> Honesty is the first chapter in the book of wisdom.
>
> —Thomas Jefferson

Quietly ask your brain what it has to say. Listen patiently, then write.

Connect with your subconscious - use your nondominant hand to write your first perception of the picture, quotes, or honesty.

Say, "_____ [your name], you are drawing your perception of honesty."

Quietly listen.

Is there anything else your brain, emotions, or spirit wish to tell you about honesty or dishonesty?

Say, "_____ [your name], you know the basis for any dishonesty.

Acknowledge dishonesty, and then let it float away."

Additional thoughts

Hope is the continuous light at the end of every dark tunnel. It will always be there when we look for it and are willing to take action to learn and grow. I can choose to walk in the darkness of hopelessness or the light of acceptance, joy, and wellbeing – hope.

Hope is important because it can make the present moment less difficult to bear. If we believe that tomorrow will be better, we can bear a hardship today

—Thich Nhat Hanh

HOPE

Hope can be a double-edged sword—unrealistic expectations versus trusting all will be well when I move into acceptance of the truth.

> Your joy, and your wellbeing is actually one of the most powerful tools you can use to change the world.
>
> —Marita Esteva 2022

Quietly ask your brain what it has to say. Listen patiently, then write

Connect with your subconscious – use your nondominant hand to write your first perception of the picture, quotes, or hope.

Say, "_____ [your name], you are drawing your perception of hope."

Quietly Listen

Is there anything else your brain, emotions, or spirit wish to tell you about hope or hopelessness?

Say, "_____[your name], you know the basis for hopelessness.

Acknowledge hopelessness, and then let it float away."

Additional thoughts:

Faith encourages me to act with trust and let go of the outcome. With faith and acceptance, I have found that fear or doubt dissipates and taking an action is much easier.

If you take the first step in faith, the others come easier.

George Sweeting 1972

Faith

I have faith that the combination of my brain, emotions, and sprit/inner knowing have my best interests at heart and will support me in my next right action when I ask. Sometimes it truly does take a conscious and mindful leap of faith.

Faith as defined by Thesaurus.com - belief that is not based on proof.

Quietly ask your brain what it has to say. Listen patiently, then write

Connect with your subconscious - use your nondominant hand to write your first perception of the picture, quotes, or faith.

Say, "_____ [your name], you are drawing your perception of faith."

Quietly listen.

Is there anything else your brain, emotions, or spirit wish to tell you about faith or doubt?

Say, "_____[your name], you know the basis for doubt. Acknowledge doubt, and then let it float away."

Additional thoughts:

Courage is the base of all decisions because it includes all my feelings and allows me to set them free. It also allows me to walk with my fears and not be run by them. A true gift.

> I learned that courage was not the absence of fear, but the triumph over it. The brave man is not he who does not feel afraid, but he who conquers that fear.
>
> —Nelson Mandela 1995

COURAGE

Being different or feeling less than takes courage. When I meet courage and walk through this fear, I am blessed. I can then be open to learning without self-judgment or concern about what others think.

If you have the courage to begin, you have the courage to succeed.

—David Viscott

Quietly ask your brain what it has to say. Listen patiently, then write

Connect with your subconscious - use your nondominant hand to write your perception of the picture, quotes, or courage.

Say, "_____ [your name], you are drawing your perception of courage."

Quietly listen.

Is there anything else your brain, emotions, or spirit wish to tell you about courage or fear?

Say, "_____ [your name], you know the basis for fear.

Acknowledge fear, and then let it float away."

Additional thoughts:

Integrity, as well as honor, honesty, and decency (synonyms for integrity), are how I want to show up in my life day by day. I want to live with kindness and compassion for Brenda and everyone else. With gratitude, I continue to learn.

When you are able to maintain your own highest standards of integrity—regardless of what others may do—you are destined for greatness.

—Napoleon Hill 1997

INTEGRITY

Integrity is being truthful within myself about my feelings, needs, and wants and where they come from. It's also letting go of unrealistic expectations of Brenda and of others.

> To give real service you must add something which cannot be bought or measured with money and that is sincerity and integrity.
> —Donald A Adams 1926

Quietly ask your brain what it has to say. Listen patiently, then write

Use your nondominant hand to write your first perception of the picture, quotes, or integrity.

Say, "_____ [your name], you are drawing your perception of integrity."

Quietly listen.

Is there anything else your brain, emotions, or spirit wish to tell you about integrity or deceit?

Say, "_____ [your name], you know the basis for deceit.

Acknowledge deceit, and then let it float away."

Additional thoughts

I have the gift of willingness when I choose to walk in the light of love and acceptance of Brenda as I am today and of others as they are. No fixing of others is necessary. I have the wonderful choice to change my attitude just for today, one day at a time.

> If you have these two things—the willingness to change, and the acceptance of everything as it comes, you will have all you need to work with.
>
> —Charlotte Selver

WILLINGNESS

A synonym of willingness is consent. Life is better for me when I consent to what is, learn about my feelings, and decide how I might want to show up in the world.

> Character, the willingness to accept responsibility for one's own life, is the source from which self-respect springs.
>
> —Joan Didion

Quietly ask your brain what it has to say. Listen patiently, then write

Connect with your subconscious - use your nondominant hand to write your first perception of the picture, quotes, or willingness.

Say, "_____ [your name], you are drawing your perception of willingness."

Quietly listen.

Is there anything else your brain, emotions, or spirit wish to tell you about willingness or unwillingness?

Say, "_____ [your name], you know the basis for unwillingness.

Acknowledge unwillingness, and then let it float away."

Additional thoughts:

Humility is about being selfless rather than self-focused. I strive to be willing to make mistakes and learn from them with honesty and grace. Being teachable at all times – oh my, what there is to learn about me and my relationship with the world around me.

Definition from Thesaurus.com
modest opinion or estimate of one's own importance. . .

HUMILITY

Being humble is letting go of ego and self for my good, our good, and the highest good of all. It's about learning to be the best I can be for others without fanfare or praise. The beauty and humility of nature is all around us.

> Where there is patience and humility, there is neither anger nor vexation.
> —Francis of Assisi

Quietly ask your brain what it has to say. Listen patiently, then write

Connect with your subconscious - use your nondominant hand to write your first perception of the picture, quotes, or humility.

Say, "_____ [your name], you are drawing your perception of humility."

Quietly listen.

Is there anything else your brain, emotions, or spirit wish to tell you about humility or pride?

Say, "_____ [your name], you know the basis for pride.

Acknowledge pride, and then let it float away."

Additional thoughts:

Self-discipline is one of my guides for living in the present and letting go of excess, resentments, and so much more. It encourages me to walk in gratitude with insight, joy, and discernment. There is nothing harsh about self-discipline for me, it gives me the gift of freedom.

Synonyms from Thesaurus.com
prudence, sobriety, determination

SELF-DISCIPLINE

Self-discipline equals self-love, self-awareness, and being in the moment. I have a choice to be a victim or an advocate of self-discipline. I choose to have a calm mind today.

> Compassion, tolerance, forgiveness and a sense of self-discipline are qualities that help us lead our daily lives with a calm mind.
> —Dalai Lama

Quietly ask your brain what it has to say. Listen patiently, then write

Connect with your subconscious - use your nondominant hand to write your first perception of the picture, quotes, or self-discipline.

Say, "_____ [your name], you are drawing your perception of self-discipline."

Quietly listen.

Is there anything else your brain, emotions, or spirit wish to tell you about self-discipline or excess?

Say, "_____ [your name], you know the basis for excess. Acknowledge excess, and then let it float away."

Additional thoughts:

Accepting myself as I am, and others as they are, is genuine and honest love. For me, this takes practice every day with brain, emotion, and spiritual awareness. My hope is that the ripple effect of the love and acceptance I send out into the world will make a difference to someone.

Have we let ourselves love the people around us, our family, our community, the earth upon which we live? And did we also learn to let go?
—Jack Kornfield

LOVE

Love—being present and authentic with Brenda and others. Walking in the light of spiritual awareness, honesty, and acceptance. Seeing others without judgment as they are. Actions and ways of thinking I do to spread love.

> The spiritual journey is the unlearning of fear and the acceptance of love.
> —Marianne Williamson

Quietly ask your brain what it has to say. Listen patiently, then write

Connect with your subconscious - use your nondominant hand to write your first perception of the picture, quotes, or love.

Say, "_____ [your name], you are drawing your perception of love."

Quietly listen.

Is there anything else your brain, emotions, or spirit wish to tell you about love or resentment?

Say, "_____ [your name], you know the basis for resentment.

Acknowledge resentment, and then let it float away."

Additional thoughts:

Perseverance, persistence, and putting one foot in front of the other remind us to follow our dreams with care, compassion, and determination. It really is up to each of us to fully live our own unique lives.

Someday, beyond the clouds and all the world's wrongs, there will be love, compassion and justice, and we shall all understand.
—Flavia Weedn

Perseverance

When I am diligent about my self-awareness journey, answers to questions or concerns seem to come more easily.

> The greatest oak was once a little nut who held its ground.
>
> —Anonymous

Quietly ask your brain what it has to say. Listen patiently, then write

Connect with your subconscious - use your nondominant hand to write your first perception of the picture, quotes, or perseverance.

Say, "_____ [your name], you are drawing your perception of perseverance."

Quietly listen.

Is there anything else your brain, emotions, or spirit wish to tell you about perseverance or quitting?

Say, "_____ [your name], you know the basis for quitting.

You are letting quitting float away."

Additional thoughts:

Spiritual Awareness comes when I practice mindful gratitude each day. This increases my self and other awareness and moves me out of my ego. I can then embrace all life has to offer – the gifts and the challenges. The challenges are gifts & lessons waiting to be recognized.

> The only way we are really going to make the future work is by allowing others to do their 'own thing' in their own way.
> —Anthon St Maarten 2016

SPIRITUAL AWARENESS

Move out of ego to embrace your spiritual connection with a higher power as you know it. There is no one right way to accomplish this connection. The more spiritually aware I am the more I am able to walk in acceptance of others as they are.

> Meditation quiets conscious thought and the physical realm, making a doorway to spiritual awareness.
>
> —Jenna Alatari

Quietly ask your brain what it has to say. Listen patiently,
then write

Connect with your subconscious - use your nondominant hand to write your first perception of the picture, quotes, or spiritual awareness.

Say, "_____ [your name], you are drawing your perception of spiritual awareness."

Quietly listen.

Is there anything else your brain, emotions, or spirit wish to tell you about spiritual awareness or ego (apathy, unconsciousness)?

Say, "_____ [your name], you know the basis for ego/apathy/unconsciousness.

You are letting ego/apathy/unconsciousness float away."

Additional thoughts:

Freely giving of ourselves to others without any expectations is a wonderful gift to all involved. The opportunities to learn self-awareness are endless when we offer, listen, and then act. Being of service can connect your brain, emotions, and spirit. Discover your service connection.

> If you want to feel connected to your own purpose, know this for certain: Your purpose will only be found in service to others, and in being connected to the something far greater than your mind/body/ego.
>
> —Wayne Dyer

SERVICE

An act of kindness given freely from the spirit and heart may go a long way in healing ourselves and others. We know not how far the ripple of this one act may travel

The best way to find yourself is to lose yourself in the service of others.
—Mahatma Gandhi

Quietly ask your brain what it has to say. Listen patiently, then write

Connect with your subconscious - use your nondominant hand to write your first perception of the picture, quotes, or service.

Say, "_____ [your name], you are drawing your perception of service."

Quietly listen.

Is there anything else your brain, emotions, or spirit wish to tell you about service or disservice?

Say, "_____ [your name], you know the basis for disservice.

You are letting disservice float away."

Additional thoughts:

What lies behind us and what lies ahead of us are tiny matters compared to what lives within us.

—Henry David Thoreau

You have completed this Discovery Is Recovery self-reflection. Living in self-awareness is not stagnant. More journals are being created to enhance your ongoing discovery journey.

May you continue to add depth, breadth, and color to your honesty, hope, faith, courage, integrity, willingness, humility, self-discipline, love, perseverance, spiritual awareness, and service as you walk your self-awareness and discovery path.

GRATITUDE

My journey in creating the Discovery Is Recovery series was much easier due to the amazing service of many. I hold deep gratitude for those in my life who reviewed various chapters and gave me their honest thoughts. There are too many to list—they know who they are. I have expanded my own self-awareness along the way thanks to each of them.

Those on the following pages freely shared encouragement, ideas, technical help, introductions to key people, cost estimates, and much more.

Arlene R. Taylor, PhD—Realizations Inc. www.realizationsinc.com

Cathryn Charette, LMFT, MS
www.psychologytoday.com/us/therapists/cathryn-camilla-charette-eureka-ca/767049

Christi Corradi—coach and art therapist
www.masteringtheartoflife.com

Hay House, Balboa Press, Hay House Writers Community

Jessica Hadari, Business Coach
OpulentPriestess.com

John Freedom, CEHP
FREA: Finding Recovery and Empowerment from Abuse
www.frea.support
www.johnfreedom.com

Julie Schlander, CHC, NLP
certified health coach and NLP master practitioner
www.healthylivingwithjulie.com

Kari Joly' Estill
Joly' Vita Bookkeeping and Consulting www.calendly.com/
karijolyestill

Patricia A. Mayer
patriciamayerlaw.com

Susan Shloss, certified money coach
susan@moneywisdomcoach.com
moneywisdomcoach.com

WendyFilbenPhotography.com
(Brenda's back cover photo)

Meet the Author

Brenda L Balding MA has lived by spiritual principles most of her life, expanded by her experiences, Master's degree, and PhD work.

Brenda resides in Northern California, where she deepens her spiritual practice through journaling, meditation, and photography. Over the past 40 years, she noticed that her photos of the natural world speak to her and others on brain, emotion, and spirit levels. She includes her images in the hope that they may facilitate deep discovery for you as they have for her.

Choosing to show up each day with compassion, acceptance, and an open willingness to learn, and expand self-awareness, enhances her inner life. Being of service adds depth and exhilaration to each day, which led to the creation of the "Discovery Is Recovery" Focused Journals.

Brenda believes that discovery leads to recovery from whatever challenges that may exist in life—for your good, our good, and the highest good of all.

Continue to walk your path of discovery.

APPENDIX

In the next pages are some mental, emotional, and spiritual modalities that many have found helpful on their journey of self-discovery.

Archetype work for spiritual, emotional, financial, and other issues provides interesting ways to get to know yourself from these perspectives. We are all multifaceted beings. Learning more about these facets can be enlightening. Research various sites. You may find some helpful along your journey.

Emotional freedom technique (EFT), or tapping, has assisted me in releasing anxiety, relaxing my body, being more present, and sleeping better. There are many professionals who offer EFT programs for healing.

Meditation, visualization, and mirror work have helped many.

Arlenetaylor.org Realizations Inc website has information about the brain and innate giftedness site Realizations Inc. The site has lots to discover—current brain research, good stories, puzzles to challenge your brain, and great recipes to support your brain and body. There are also books for children to stimulate their brain-emotion-spirit connection, and for you as you read the stories.

The twelve-step way of life, developed by Alcoholics Anonymous, has given the gift of brain-emotion-sprit connection to many experiencing any obsession of the mind/brain, emotions, and spirit.

Yoga, tai chi, qigong, and others may assist with accessing your brain-body connection and expanding your spiritual awareness.

<hr />

Use the following page to note what you have found helpful on your discovery journey. Be open and listen to your brain, emotions, and spirit. Find what works for you.

NOTES

The book you have just created is some of your story and may lead you on a new path of discovery or writing. This is truly about your life journey. Be open, listen, and be willing to take a leap of faith as Brenda did.

Continue to emerge into your true, loving, resilient, shining way of being as you connect your brain, emotion, and spirit for your good, our good, and the highest good of all. Blessings to each of you.

Check out more of the "Discovery Is Recovery" Focused Journals, coming soon.

Be well and enjoy your full and amazing life!

> A journey of a thousand miles must begin with a single step.
>
> —Lao-tzu

Printed in the United States
by Baker & Taylor Publisher Services